A Different Point of View

Hampton R. Olfus, Jr.

Cover and Illustrations by Hampton R.Olfus, Jr.

Also by Horace Mungin

Sleepy Willie Talks about Life
Sleepy Willie Sings the Blues
The Devil Beats His Wife
San Juan Hill
Subway: After the Irish
Poetic Portraits: The African People of San Jun Hill

These books can be ordered at:
www.Hmunginbooks.com
(843) 437-7567

For wholesale orders:
Horace Mungin Books
152 McArn Road
Ridgeville, SC 29472
(843) 875-3886

To Einstein

What could I do?
What-could-I-do?

I got all choked up
And put down my gun
I called him my pa
And he called me his son
And I came away with
A different point of view.

FROM: A BOY NAMED SUE - JOHNNY CASH

Contents

CONTENTS

Authors Note

In 1968 my brother Ted and I formed *"Brothers Publishing Company."* We published two chapbooks of my early poetry, *Dope Hustler's Jazz* ('68) and *"Now See Here, Homes"* ('69). Until now theses were my only published poetry collections. Those early poems were written nearly on the spot. They were my rough reactions to the turbulent events of the sixties. My real literary activism started in 1970 with the creation of *"Black Forum Magazine."* I found the magazine with four other writers, Charles Pole, Revish Windham, Fred Richardson and Julia Coaxum to be a medium where young black writers could dialogue with each other, share the writing experience and improve their skills. I was the magazine's first editor and I stayed with it for 5 years. During this time we published the works of hundreds of writers and poets and we featured revealing profiles and interviews with established literary figures like John Oliver Killens, Nikki Grimes, Louise Meriwether and Amiri Baraka. The Magazine had a writers' workshop and a writers' market place. We produced readings and literary events around the city. This is where I sharpened my literary advocacy and activism. In 1980, I founded a literary newsletter called *"Press Time"* with my wife Gussie, we did much of the same things as *Black Forum*, but our contact with our writer/subscribers was more intimate – this was more of a virtual writers' workshop with essential exchanges in each issue. I was learning poetry as I was learning the literary business. These experiences invigorated my ability as a poet and nurtured my skills, but they also fostered my instinct to share.

Thirty years later I met a talented young writer and historian in Charleston, SC who was surprised at my eagerness to share with him what I knew about writing – he didn't know then that this was my nature, I couldn't help myself - this is what I'm about.

The poems in this book were written over a forty-seven year period, between 1965 and 2012. They are arranged in two sections. The first section I call *The Reconstruction*. The poems in this section represent the era when my literary universe was formulating anew 1979 to the present. This reframing of my mind-set started a decade or so after the end of legal segregation in the South and the establishment of a handful of national laws to protect the civil rights of African Americans. This was also when restrictions on black people in *almost* every field of endeavor started crumbling down. During this time, America, and Americans, made modest efforts and produced moderate gains in improved racial conditions and racial relations. A time when, for me, the question of race (though still a huge problem) declined as the number one issue in America. This change was so gradual that my swing in literary focus was imperceptible. During this time I also moved my focus to prose writing. I continued to write poems now and then, some of which were published in journals and other publications, but for the most part, these poems were written because they were inspired by some seminal event and not composed purposely to go into a pending collection, so they were completed and then filed away.

During the intervening time (40 years), I wrote 6 books. The sixth book was a kind of poetry book. It was a collection of what I call "*Poetic Portraits*" of people I grew up with in the Amsterdam Projects in New York City. The year I spent submerged in the poetry of that project nudged me towards looking at the poetry file I had compiled over the years. Reading over a dozen or so of these poems dating from 1965 I noticed a stark difference in the earlier poems from the ones written after the 1980's. Although black liberation was still my overall theme, I had moderated on methods to liberation and the degree to which I focused on systematic racism. While the earlier poems were rebellious "Power to the People" tirades against the system of racial injustice, the later works strongly pointed out inequalities but they seem to accept politics, time and re-education as a practical means to a just future.

I was stunned and thought the difference important enough to share. I decided to put a collection of those poems together. The title was obvious to me – *A Different Point of View.* These poems represent a viewpoint evolving in direct correlation to the racial changes taking place in America. All of this brought me to the reality that I saw America in another light. I had formed a different point of view about America's heretofore intransigent on the matter of racial injustices. The America I experience from birth was yielding. This America which shaped my mistrust of it during the sixties when I realized that its oppression of black people was deliberate, thorough and transparent was collapsing under the pressure of the Civil Rights Movement. This new reality reflected itself in what I wrote – these poems are like a record of the transformation of America. The poems written during the period that I called *The Reconstruction* are not all about race, but I mention the volatility of the American racial difficulties to bring to mind the background in which these poems were constructed and where the change is most vivid.

I believe that all the poems in this collection are interesting, well written and provocative, but what makes this a note-worthy collection is that the reader can follow the transformation that took place over a forty year period. The moderation in the later poems can be directly traced to the racial moderation that's taking place in America. With all the racial dust being kicked up during and after the recent 2012 presidential election, it can easily seem that there has been no change at all, but step back a moment to realized that the racism coming out today is background noise to the results of an election involving a black president – this isn't an issue we confronted in say, 1952, 62, 72, or 82. This is a clear shift in the battlefield.

The second section of the book is called *The Insurrection*. The poems in this section represent the period of the movement – the turbulent sixties, when individuals and organizations were rebelling against America's culture of racism. During this time I tried to form words into poems that described, encouraged, or aided the insurrection. This is how I was made to feel that I was a part of the movement by having it shape my thinking and my literature. My absorption of the movement became my contribution to it. It changed my life. That, after all, was the goal of the movement – to change all of our lives, enabling us to survive the period with stiffened backs, a new reality and a different point of view. The movement's success, in my case, is evident to the degree to which I have come to express this different point of view. So in a sense, the reader is traveling back through my literary development to the first poem of mine to appear in a major publication. That poem was "My Thing" published on Tuesday, April 25, 1969 in *The New York Times*, from my first chapbook "Dope Hustler's Jazz". The poem was described as expressing an ideal of personal liberation "characteristic" of the poetry being produced by poets of the Black Arts Movement during that time. During the journey back through the decade of *The Insurrection*, the reader will discover what I mean by *"A Different Point of View."*

America has changed in fifty years. We all have changed to some degree. I have selected poems (published and unpublished) for this section that I hoped would recreate the feel of the time that represented *The Insurrection*. I want readers old enough to remember that time; to relive the period and recapture that fire. I want readers who are not old enough to remember the period, to experience it, perhaps, for the first time here in the poems in this book. I want this book to put into perspective some of the elements that changed America to the point where the election of Barack Obama as president of the United States became possible, so that we can reignite that fire. And together, we shall all arrive at this new juncture in the continued struggle for justice with a different point of view.

The cover and all the illustrations in this book are by Hampton R. Olfus Jr. Brother Hampton is a Washington DC native, who grew up in Prince Georges County, MD., in the town of Glenarden. He started drawing about the age of four, and sold his first painting by the time he was 13 years old. Hampton studied art while attending, Prince George's Community College in Largo, MD., and continued his studies after college. His works has been exhibited far beyond the DC area. He now lives in North Charleston, S.C. Since his arrival in Charleston in 2009, his works has been exhibited at the College of Charleston, Avery Research Center, Galliard Auditorium, North Charleston Gallery, Moja Juried Art Exhibition, and the Charleston Artist Guild Gallery. Brother Hampton sees his career as an artist as "a journey of a life force expressing itself through the human experience." Some of his works has elements of Aaron Douglas and William Henry Johnson, artists from the Harlem Renaissance period

The 14 drawings in this book could stand well on their own in an exhibition in any art galleries in this country or any other. After you've read the poems and seen the drawing as a whole, I invite you to go back through the book viewing only the art drawings and experience the congruity each piece has to the other. There is a consistency in their quality as well as in the story they tell – gallery owners would do well to seek this artist out. I am extremely fortunate for his collaboration on this book and profoundly hopeful for our future partnership.

Horace Mungin

The Reconstruction

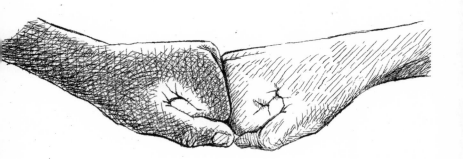

The Water Fountain

I know that you wouldn't want me to bring this up
And I wonder why that is, could it be your shame,
Your vanity, your regret or your guilt
When you are made to remember these circumstances
You lay the blame down to another generation
To assign culpability on your ancestors
You disown their evil exploits without disowning them
Or that you spring from them as inheritor of the privileges
Their enforced supremacy created for them and for you

Nor do you like me to mention that it took federal laws to
Cease the practice of your advantages through oppression

Because I know that there is nothing but law;
Not your morality or your religion, nor your benevolence
Which could prevent you from resuming the practice and
Revive all the social, cultural, and economic amenities
That accompanies White Only water fountains
Once your needs arises, I stand watch over
Water fountains as the first sign of recidivism.

Searching for the Day White People in America Went Crazy

(Of all the whimsical facts of American life
There is this one certainty: White people have gone crazy)

Was it the day they purchased Manhattan
From the Indians for 24 dollars' worth
Of trinkets
Or the day the Manhattan Project Invented
The bomb and took the world hostage forever

Was it the day colonist in Boston refused
To concede to the Tea Act Tax or the day
The Tea Party rallied to support the Bush
Tax cuts for the richest Americans

Was it the day the first slave ship left
The Door of No Return or was it the day
Garvey purchased the S.S. Yarmouth and
Rechristen it the S.S. Frederick Douglass or
The day O.J. Simpson was acquitted

Searching for the day white people in America went crazy

Was it the day secessionists convened the Constitutional
Convention to establish the Confederacy or the day
John Brown raided Harpers Ferry or the day
The National Voting Rights Act was signed into law
Or the day Martin Luther King, Jr.
Went to the balcony of the Lorraine Hotel

Was it when millions of shackled souls
Were loss to the Middle Passage or
At the battle of Gettysburg where
Thousands from the north and

A Different Point of View

More thousands from the south
Laid their burdens down
Or the evening Lincoln went to the theater or
Was it while watching Birth of a Nation

Was it the day the Monroe doctrine set out
The goals of gunboat diplomacy making the
World ripe for American exploitation or
The day robber-barons purchased American politicians
Creating the need for money counting machines
Or the day John D. Rockefeller covered for
The oligarchy by throwing dimes to the poor

Searching for the day white people in America went crazy

Was it the day Custer took a stand at Little Big Horn
Or the day the Turner Diaries were written or
The day Timothy McVeigh took a trip to Oklahoma City
Or the creation of the Aryan Republican Army
Was it the day the great depression began or
The day taxpayers bailed out Wall Street while
Millions in bonuses went to stock manipulators or
The day the government enacted the Affordable Care Act

Or

Was it the day Barack Obama walked from Kenya through
Northern Africa and Eastern Europe to Russia to collect his
Communist credentials then stopped in Germany to gain his
Hitler appeal before walking the Atlantic Ocean to America
And the White House where he proclaimed himself President
Of the United States and Commander-in-Chief of its
military

Or was it the day a decorated army officer disobeyed
Legal orders because he regarded the Commander-in-Chief
As illegitimate and not an American

Was it the day the entire Republican leadership said No
To America because they wanted this Kenyan to fail
Even if this brought the American people down with him
Or was it the day Fox News organized protesters who
Portrayed Obama as Hitler and called him a socialist or
The day they gathered at the White House carrying signs
That read: *We didn't bring our guns this time*
Or was it the day they brought their guns to Washington

Birthers say Obama is not American born
Others say he is the Anti-Christ
Fox News promote him as a Muslim
White people are smart enough to know
When they have been deceived, they have figured it out:
Barack Obama hoodwinked
The entire American establishment
Its system of checks and balances
Its national security apparatus
Its southern intelligentsia on matters of race
Its white man-in-the-street barometer
To hijacked America and now they want their country back
Even if it takes Second Amendment remedies
They want their country back.

Searching for the day white people in America went crazy.

One Energy

I have come to understand my connection to you
And to the oceans, the mountains and the trees
And to the sun, the moon and to the stars;
To my thoughts and to my actions and to all
Creation - we are all one energy

When we look into my fragments we see
Your atoms which in infinity manifests as
Sub-atomic matter - particles that are
Photons, leptons, electrons, neutrons, quarks
The fundamental building blocks of nature -
All of the all

Everything that exists in the entire cosmos,
Which is experienced with the five physical senses
From the infinitely large to the infinitely small,
From the macroscopic to the microscopic
Consisted of sub-atomic particles which at their core
Are comprised of this one pure energy

These particles form to attract additional particles
That harmonizes with their vibrational match
Which transmutes from the quantum field
To become the physical things that can be seen -
The physics world of matter and stuff

Communication between energy is not
Subject to time and space
The entire cosmos is a huge vibrating ball
Of interconnected endless energy with the ability
To communicate into eternity with no regard
To space and time and what this energy joins together
Is based only on our individual thoughts
Which means you already know all of this

Life is about finding that which you already know
And settling in amid the eternally familiar places.

Juba Zulu

Juba Zulu
Makes me long for home
The home of my father's father father's father
And the old rituals of a peaceful time
And a timeless place
And Jomo on a grassy knoll minded the cattle
And the old men each noon cadenced a different chant
To please the spirits of our ancestors

Jaboo/jaboo/jaha/jaha/jaboo/jaboo/jaha/jaha

Juba Zulu
Spirit of my father's father father's father
Forgive us for our corrupt ways
And guide us back to your ways
And the dundun drum
And songs of praise for our ancestors
And the talking drums which speaks
The truth of the great One

Juba Zulu
Great ancestral spirit
You once taught my father's father father's father
The rituals of the wind and the sea and the earth
And to run with the gazelles
While the elder's chanted intercessions

Jaboo/jaboo/jaha/jaha/jaboo/jaboo/jaha/jaha

Juba Zulu
Makes me long for home
And the reach of other possibilities
And my father's brother is my father
And my father's brother's son is my brother

7

And my neighbor is my brother
And everyone is known one to the other as brother
And Jomo brings the cattle home
At dusk for bleeding and millet

Juba Zulu
I would like to see the elders
Under the tropical evergreens
The mahogany
And the ebony trees
Eating kola nuts
And rubbing palm oil
And chanting in the old ancestral cadence

Jaboo/jaboo/jaha/jaha/jaboo/jaboo/jaha/jaha.

A Prayer for Tsunami Victims

Nam Myoho Renge Kyo
Nam Myoho Renge Kyo
Nam Myoho Renge Kyo

In a village where each generation fished the sea
For a century taking what made for their livelihood
The sea was a benevolent friend
The sea was a bountiful and giving servant
The sea was mother to all beyond the distant vista

Nam Myoho Renge Kyo

Reflecting the glare of the early morning sun
Providing a practical means of transportation
Village to village, port to port
An alluring portrait with the moon
On its horizon this giving servant
Of commerce and esthetic – the sea

Nam Myoho Renge kyo

Then for the first time in a century
The sea disturbed by the thrust of tectonic plates
Elevated and moved with undeniable force
Towards that village and that land – Japan
Sweeping up everything in its path
Boats, homes, cars, electric poles, toys
People and fishing nets
Leaving hundreds homeless awaiting
News of family and neighbors among the
Tens of thousands unaccounted for
And not yet on the list of survivors or
Until the sea returns to the shores

A Different Point of View

All the bodies it so violently ripped away
We offer our tears, we offer this prayer

Nam Myoho Renge Kyo
Nam Myoho Renge Kyo
Nam Myoho Renge Kyo

The Boy Next Door

They whispered behind his back
Said things children shouldn't hear
Because he was tall and lean and had the
Gracefulness of Alvin Ailey but
He never troubled anybody just
Danced his dance taking the world for a twirl

They were astonished by his theatrical range
And thought him as freakiest as the
Characters he portrayed - who does he
Think he is – Charles Laughton?
That boy never troubled anybody
His talent was real natural

Women loved to wallow platonically
In his splendidly dreamy Sal Mineo eyes
And mimic his sometimes sassy manner
He was generous with fashion hints and
Was bubbled over champagne among them
But he never trouble anyone just
Shared his joy for life

He could be impish like Truman Capote
Or gloomy as Montgomery Clift
Silky as Johnnie Mathis
Smart as Barney Frank
And popular as Harvey Milk and
That boy never troubled anybody merely
Wanted the world to accept his worth

He made a ghost appearance in James Baldwin's
Giovanni's Room but all they saw was sin and
Every religion called him shameful
He was as deeply rooted in the community

A Different Point of View

As Langston Hughes cared for people so
That boy never troubled anyone just
Knew that he was made in the first creation

Last week when I heard that he was robbed
Beaten and left for dead, oh I know what
Had caused it one those graceless men acted out
One them unholy phobia's even though
That boy never troubled anyone just came
Into the world as God would have him.

An Act of Worship

For Alluette

You are the dreamer that was born
To open new vistas to the holistic
Possibilities and become Queen of a universal soul food
That passion for the culinary arts passed down
From a grandfather who cooked in the military
And a grandmother who loved cooking, gardening,
Flowers and everything beautiful -
Evolving to form the melody in your nature
To dine in your presence is an act of worship

You are the dreamer who was raised
In the Old Village of Mount Pleasant
But left home after High School
Because that is what you do to grow
To find the song in your heart and
To let that song sing a remembrance
Of the evolution that happens in your journey
To dine in your presence in an act of worship

You are the dreamer born knowing that
You would not toil long in the vineyard of others
You inherited your father's entrepreneurial spirit
To establish the Line Street Grill and Grocery
It was there that you found your heart's song
In your own vineyard and all the components
Of your existence sung in unison
And there you built your future in that sentiment
To dine in your presence is an act of worship

You are the dreamer whose friends all know your
Affinity for a party on your birthday
They come because they know you embrace
The philosophy that says

A Different Point of View

You are what you eat
And they come to taste and witness at the
Altar of your knowledge of smart foods
That pleases the eyes, delights the palate
And nourishes the body and mind
To dine in your presence is an act of worship

You are the dreamer; when your time came
To fight for survival you choose your
Birthday to have the surgery
If you were to seek the secrets death holds
You wanted it to be on your birthday
And as it turns out this mystery resides
In the heart of life and living – you are here - now
All these years after – a tower in the storm
A way in the darkness
And to dine in your presence is an act of worship

They are the many, the rich and the famous
The young and the old
The gifted and the common
The rainbow
Who come to sing your praises and
Wish you well in your goal
That by a positive attitude, nourishing foods,
Pure water, exercise and prayers, you will
Live to double your current age.

To dine in your presence in an act of worship.

God Blessed America

God gave us Colin Powell
To remind us how things use to be
For a black man in government
Boundless expectations and unbearable disappointments.

God gave us Condoleezza Rice
To let us know that being a second-rate
Concert pianist is less damaging
To the order of the world then guiding
A witless president through the confusion
Of international diplomacy.

God gave us Donald Rumsfeld
To let us experience the bloodied
Tangled webs of war
To muddle through day after day
Year after year – always
Professing to know where the exit sign is.

God gave us Elberto Gonzales
To make us loathe servitude and
Desire integrity
And to remind us to always
Avenge the Alamo.

God gave us Dick Cheney
Because God has a sense of irony
God wants that we should learn to
Stay out of Dick Cheney's
Gunsights.

God gave us Karl Rove
With George bush on his knees
To help us develop an appreciation
For the fine art of puppetry.

A Different Point of View

And God gave us George Bush
Because God loves us and God knows
That the America Bush constructs
Will finally wake us up and God wants
That we should all finally wake up.

The America We See In the Malls

It's on cable television and talk radio
This bluster of shackled demons
Desperately clinking to Jim Crow's yesteryear
And the disposition of 1930's America

They come from ancient cemeteries
With archaic points of views
To halt gays, banish emigrants
Discontinued the social compact with
The elderly and the disadvantaged
Stop social advancements
Undo all perceived threats
To the survival of the status-quo

Their outrage is so widespread
That it's easy to miss the promise
Young people of all races and classes
Are committing too – a rainbow equality
That sustains itself in its actual diversity
The America we see in the malls

This future that will surely engulf the entire
American nation goes mostly unnoticed
Overshadowed by the fury of obstructionist
With a hundred reasons why the
Injustices of the past are all still unavoidable
Justice – yes, perhaps in another hundred years
Now is not the time they say

While young people forged a new
American social order of unimpeded
Compassion and fairness
Irrational phantoms only half oblivious
To the emerging new America

A Different Point of View

Chained to the corruptions of the past
Clinging to the old social order
Chant the same babbled mantra
Refrain by refrain – we want our country back

Delirious and absurdly confused
By the advent of an event though so impossible
Not even the arrival of our other selves
From a parallel universe could be as perplexing
After 232 years the American president is black
And the American senses stumble about in the darkness
Of this new experience seeking ghost of ancient times

On the surface one can hardly detect it
But look around my friends
Look around
The times, they are a changing.

Nourishment
For Aunt Viola

There was a time in the place
Where I was born
When the human spirit soared
Even under the rock of oppression
There were no words for mine
There were no words for yours
Everything belonged to everyone
In my poor hamlet of dirt and despair.

Oppression, poverty, illiteracy
And governmental bias and neglect
These things brought my village
Together sharing all
Childcare, potatoes, hammers, faith.

At breakfast we shared hope for another day
At dinner we shared a meager pot of optimism
At supper we shared the grief of yet another day
And still there were times of laughter and joy
Even to people who suffered so much for so long
God renders moments of gaiety for sharing.

And of all the things shared
In my village of dirt and needs
The thing most appreciated by me
Is my Aunt Ola's breast milk
Each upon a knee we nursed
My twin cousin and me
Neither breast his
Neither breast mine.

Cape Town Sorcerer

I was walking the streets in Cape Town, South Africa
With my wife and ten relatives from America
And our Cape Town host family
We had come for the wedding of a nephew
To their lovely daughter

Obvious tourist taking in the sights
And being observed as we observed
We passed people as curious about us
As we were about them – checking each other out
Anonymously

Then a woman; a passerby, with a light brown
Pleasant round face and a pleasing body and
Fast talking eyes that locked on to my eyes
For all so slight of a moment telling me
How much she wanted me to come to her

My eyes, as far as I can tell only
Answered that there was no hope
A transmission that I'm sure
Constituted an involuntary infidelity.

Life Partners

I was once young and looking for you
You were once young and looking too
We were both once young our hearts apart

The universe is wonder and mystery
The ordained is the ordained or did we
Meet through the quirk of possibilities
On this most horrible day for the nation
And a most wonderful day for us we will
Always remember November 22, 1963

The universe conspired to have us meet
Planned or quirk - it happened and
We took control from there to
Form this lasting bond of 50 years

The years has flown by with laughter and tears
All a seal to our commitment to this union
We raised our family to families of their own

And now in these golden years we smile
A knowing smile of confidence
Of whom we were for all these years.

The Cosmos

For Nicole

The cosmos exist in a most
Beautiful and mysterious setting
Of its self – but the cosmos
Cannot claim neither pride nor credit
For its wonderment
And if the universe viewed
A reflection of its self
It would be as astonished as
We all are
Who peer into the night sky
Or
As astonished as you
Surely are
Whenever you see
You.

Jump over the Broom

For Robert and Priscilla

The sky is bright and clear
There is a still peace in the air
Humming birds are heard all the morning long
Flowers shone more brilliant from the dawn
This is a fine day for marriage.

The sun is in your window
Your hearts are on a wing
Down deep in love's chapel
Rapture and attachment can
Find no day more suitable
For the chants at love's altar.

True love seldom beckons true lovers/
True lovers seldom meet
With the passions of romance/desire/
And the winged spirit of real commitment/
That commitment which harbors mutual dependency
While it promotes the growth of individual spirits.

And among all the gathered this day
There is the warmth of the ceremonial
Continuance of the tradition of our forefathers
Jump over the broom
Jump over the broom and make this family
Strong and indomitable.

Our presence is tribute to love
Our presence is tribute to this marriage
We know that no evil will part you
And we gather here a happy throng for you the husband
And we gather here a happy throng for you the wife
And we gather here a happy throng for ourselves

THE RECONSTRUCTION

In your union you secure our dreams
In your union you secure our traditions
In your union you secure our future.

And on your first anniversary
We will bring you paper/
And on your second anniversary
Cotton/
And on your fifth anniversary
Wood/
And on your tenth anniversary
Tin/
And on your twentieth anniversary
China/
And on you fiftieth anniversary
Gold/

This is a fine day for love and commitment
This is fine day for marriage/
This is a fine day to jump over the broom.

Bill Chatman, My Friend

First let it be said that
Bill inherited his mother's
Generosity and love of people

Then let it be said that
I was his friend and brother
Sometimes I was Cain
And he was Able

He will understand that I once
Wore the code of the malicious streets
In a triad with two others whose
Codes were cruel and self-centered
It was us against the world
Then us against each other

And at first this is what
I brought to our gentle friendship
It gave me such advantage
Over this trusting soul
Who still sucked his finger

As we did lots of things together
I eased away from my thuggish ways
To start seeing our relationship fair
By then I was so far ahead in the
Psychological support we offered each other
He recognized the disparity but in our
True friendship he never did despair

And many years went between
Us separated and out of touch
And he took the fall but got up
(I wonder had I been with him

Would I have fallen too or could
I have prevented his fall?)

His talent for cleanliness took
Him to the position of regional
Custodial manager of a chain of
McDonalds a huge accomplishment

Then the family cursed gene set in to sit
Atop the abuse he self-administered
During the fall
He lost a toe, then a foot, then most
Of a leg then on the other leg the problem
Worked to wear him down then came
The coma Ruby was always there

But our sister later told me
Of the road he traveled through
No fault of his own
And how his body rebelled
And of his years of suffering
And severed limbs

Then I went to read Kahlil Gibran
On Friendship
And had my spirits buoy
When in his writings he said:
For that which you love most in him
May be clearer in his absence
As the mountain to the climber
Is clearer from the plain

Then our sister told me
How he smiled
And willingly accepted when
He knew his hour was near.

Why?

I come from a generation of warriors
Born into a time of strife
And the wretched years of American history:
The history of backdoor inequity
The history of trees that bear strange fruits
The history of Jim Crow
The history of reconstruction
The history of slavery
The history of the middle passage
And, yes the history of kings and queens
Back home.
I come from a generation of warriors
Who valued the possibilities of struggle
And the legitimacy of our existence
A generation with an agenda, a vision
And the will to overcome the malicious
Contortions of our realities
The generation of the movement
Of sit-ins and freedom rides
Of protest marches and civil disobedience
Of conflict and confrontations
Of small and permanent victories that changed a nation
I come from a generation of dragon slayers.
I come from that generation of warriors
Who gave birth to a generation lost
The just do it generation
The BET generation
The Hip Hop generation
The drive-by shooting generation
A generation that was past the promise
Of a great and glorious future
Of greater victories until we reached a full partnership
And now we watch in horror
As they devour themselves in senseless bloodbaths

And orgies of violence and unforgivable distortions
Of what it is we passed on to them
And we like rejected suitors can only ask why?
Why? I asked an old holy man
Who is one hundred years old and lives on the Sea Island
Who learned to play chess ninety years ago
On a craved board with whittled wooden pieces
A holy man who says that this is a time of sorcerers
and demons
But who is mainly referring to the fact that he now owns
A computerized chess set that beats him more often than not
He thinks the chess set is enchanted
And was engineered by the wizards of witchcraft
He thinks the modern world is enchanted
There is too much magic the old holy man says.
Why are there guns everywhere?
.44 Magnums, Colt 45's pistols,
Berrettas, Glock 17's, Ladysmiths, Uzi's Tec 9's,
AK 47's, M1's, M2's M16's
And conflicts - like sex or, a crack pipe
Comes easy.
Why are there so many guns in the hands
Of people so eager to use them?
And death – likes cable TV or, delivered pizza
Come hot, fast and easy
What do you want on your tombstone?
Is more than a commercial slogan.
Why? A little girl in Charleston asked her father
Is the church door locked and bolted?
To protect the typewriters and the copying machine
The gold cross on the altar and the other valuables
The father answers
Well is God safe in there?
God is in there, God is out here too, God is everywhere
The fathers says feeling this isn't quite the answer
Why then is the church door locked and bolted?

A Different Point of View

The girl repeats
The father says nothing
This is not a question with a simple answer.
Raymond Otis lives in the North Charleston
He learned about the police force's gun buy-back
Program on the news
Raymond parts with his battered Beretta
To receive a valued gift certificate then
He drives Rivers Avenue to the nearest Sports Authority
And brings home to his four sons
Four like real water Uzi's
One real gun brings four toy guns into their world
To perpetuate the lore of the gun
Too much magic in the world the old holy man said.
This is the magic of the supreme architects
Of our society – ruling from their ivory towers
While breeding a generation of people so full
Of hopelessness and despair and alienation
They loathe themselves
A generation with empty hearts and
Boundless trouble
A generation whose hatred is so intense
No one is safe
No one
Not the mothers and fathers of their freedom nor
The architects of their calamity
And when the serpents reach into ivory towers
The social engineers will also cry out – why?
But what they will really want to know is
What can we do?
What can we all do?

Anatomy of a Swindle

She first declared that we were family
From so far back the linage was unclear
She seemed genuinely glad with the
Connection her eyes twinkled with delight

I got to know who she pretended she was
She secretly harbored so many
Of her frailties – that for a while I thought
Her authentic

In time she disclosed her awful history
But
In a manner which elevated her from it
(Duplicity is her nature)
She crawled from the abyss on her own in her view
And I was proud to hear what I thought
Was her story of redemption
From the beginning she flaunted her
Curious achievements the adoption
Of a white child and the mental castration
Of her husband for his infidelities

She had purposely design a carnival existence
And tried but failed to hark it on Oprah now
She employed me to write it on paper
All about her rural childhood spent in dire poverty
And her unfortunate assignment of parents
Her inability to carry a pregnancy to term
That led her to crave the white baby
Betrayals that turned her man into a eunuch in her bed
How she got her way with other men to carve out
From them a space of her own and the
Events that string these episodes together

A Different Point of View

I finished putting together these unflattering affairs
In nine long grueling months of pain and pity then
She unceremoniously seized my voice telling her story
She couldn't see how badly she underestimated me
And in the ensuing litigation I saw her true face
Both of them - but I conquered only one

The Union Man

...And the boss man brutal and mean
Sent John Brown down the hole...the abyss
I protested and I followed
   We work down in the mines
   Where the sun never shines
   And hearts never stop crying.
...And John Brown, hardworking, leader
Among workmen of the abyss – never
Complained, never grumbled, never
Rejected the boss manís favors
And I who followed lay
Trapped by rock and fire
And the boss man's lies
   Dying because we were without
   Power, without purpose, without
   Voice, without control
   Over our bones and hours.
...And surrounded by rock and fire
Down in that hole
We longed for a brighter day
And another chance to join with
Black Ivory Monroe the union man
Who feared not boss nor system
Brutal and mean...
   Monroe who spoke up to give workers
   Power and purpose and
   Control over our bones and hours.
...And John Brown and I who followed
Never returned from the abyss
For we missed our only chance to
Follow the union man.

Taylor at Five

Bollyholly agwhoa
Flippypoppen aaagahoppin
Puffyatrappy tootlebug
Stargazzingbrightensky

Tinyeinyantypanty **evil**
Alfullytallfully **rouf**
Yallwallyo **eerht**
Limpopo **owt**
Obeen **eno**
Ready

Trying to find the right words
To wish
A dear princess
A happy, happy
Birthday
Why don't I simply say
Happy birthday Taylor.

Mother

Our mothers are everything
To us and to our world
Mother is God's handmaiden
Created to fashion the world.

She is our consolation in sorrow
She is our hope in misery
She is our strength in weakness
She is our nourishment in famine.

Mother is everything
She introduces us to the world
And the world to us.

She is the source of our love
She is the source of our mercy
She is the source of our sympathy
She is the source of our forgiveness.

Everything in nature affirms
The reverence of motherhood
The sun is mother to the earth
The earth is mother to all that grows upon it.

And the mother/she was assigned
By God/to mold, raise and nurture
All existence/for she is
The eternal spirit of life
Filled with beauty and love.

Einstein and Me

When Einstein was born she brought
From the eternal cosmos that tiny
Piece of me that completed my connection
To the ageless energy of our
Sub-atomic memory
We recognized each other intuitively

Einstein is my six year-old granddaughter
Natalie of a thousand kisses and eyes
Dark and round, lovely and searching
She is the grand inquisitor for whom
Each answer presents another series of questions
Stubborn and perpetually in motion
She is a coiled atom about to burst
Into a new-age renaissance

Her mind as busy as Galileo's
She forges ahead in play in a
Chaotic storm – busybody attraction
That encompasses all her surroundings
Harnessed – this anarchy will
Shape her future brilliance

She brings a kind of joy
I never knew existed with a hug
And a thousand kisses and
The gaze of an explorer

Grandpa you got some
Of the most amazing things
She says
As she survey the contents of

A Different Point of View

My office
Where later I write this poem

Thank you Einstein
I say,
For letting me see
The rest of me –

Syncopation
For Patti

Pure grace is her every
Gesture
A wave, a shrug, a nod
All movements of elegant poise
Motion syncopation
Scott Joplin's sound
Lives when she moves...and
Awkwardness begs mercy.

The History of New Music in America (??)

The first sound was the lament of the drum.
The second sound was a wail across the ocean.
The third sound was a cry of disorientation.
The fourth sound was a telling silence.
The fifth sound was a sad hum of adaptation.

Born to a new soil
A new music
An American music.

A music that spoke directly to on High
For sustenance to keep the spirit
Unyielding to odious burdens
Naked and conquered, music is the only
Shield and the only weapon.

From on High came a new tongue
A sacred sound against tyranny
A spear in the heart of oppression
A spiritual tongue to beseech the All Mighty
A survival tongue that told the secret
Of the North Star.

Born to a new soil
A new music
An American music.

The sixth sound was the yell of exhilaration.
The seventh sound was the cheer of creativity.
The eight sound was the blending of traditions.
The ninth sound was the gust of optimism.
The tenth sound was the birth of syncopation.

THE RECONSTRUCTION

A music that fortified the soul during bondage
Now buttress the spirit with hope for the future
And the gaiety of the cakewalk crossed boundaries
Paving the path for the New Negro to come
Who prayed thank You Lord
Your rock of music has held us to your bosom.

A music sprouted legs and walked then ran
Through the South and up the Mississippi
The poetry of the blues steeped
In human suffering and resolve
While ragtime chronicled a graceful sound
And an eloquent tempo
This music will conquer the conqueror
The Queen of England danced the cakewalk
And the great migration north begun.

The lament of the drum and
The wail across the ocean and
The cry of disorientation and
The telling silence and
The sad hum of adaptation and
The yell of exhilaration and
The wheel of creativity and
The blending of tradition and
The gust of optimism and
The birth of syncopation
All branched out like a mighty nurturing tree.

Born to a new soil
A new music
An American music.

An alienated traumatized music traveled
North for jobs and a chance to participate
In the political process

And then the jitter-bug and the boogie-woogie
Happy feet stomping at the Savoy
All this from the lament of the drum
All this from the wail across the ocean.

The world came back from war the second time
And the big band swung/swinging again
Jim Crow and low paying jobs in the north
Lynching and segregation in the south
And there was music to tell those stories
There was also a music that fought back.

The blues took on rhythm
And gave birth to Doo Wop
And the movement was on
And Bebop turned cool
And took a freedom ride
And the Motown resonance was the
Sound track to the revolution in the streets
And cool jazz went abstract
To examine organized chaos
And there were gun-toting
Panthers making the music real

For a future generation of hip hoppers
All this from the lament of the drum
All this from the wail across the ocean.

Born to a new soil
A new music
An American music.

What is Time

Wake up, wake up, it's the New Year
That moment which is the same moment
When you were in the old year.

Time travels like a horse and buggy
Or the years fold into each other
Like an accordion or like a movement
So fast its sound is left behind

Are the edges of time beginning and end
All amassed at all the same time
As we move through the space of a time
Already in existence

Travel back to the beginning of time
The big bang and witness that you can
Go no further because before then
Time did not exist

Wake up, wake up, it's the New Year
Everyday all the same time.

Jazz

Hey baba Rebop
Baba Rebop
Cut a rug
Jitterbug
Boogie
Boogie Woogie
Rag Mop
Pooper stopper
Bugaloo
Rusty Dusty
Bebop
Sporty Odity
Hip-Hop
Didity Bopper
Rag Mop
Bebop
Hip-Hop.

Thelonious Monk on Amsterdam Avenue

Sounds of the movement of life fill the unseen
Spaces of New York City as elsewhere but listen here
To New York City's Amsterdam Avenue
On Sixty-Fourth Street

Life resonates differently during the recurring
Cycles of summer and winter/day and night
Sounds are dissimilar in the morning from noon
To evening and 'round midnight
Echoes of the rhythms of life set to an uneven tempo
This cacophony of sounds emanating
From the energy of our animation

The street is filled with the sounds of traffic
Automobile engines make a sundry noise
Horns shriek an irregular cadence
Hundreds of tires peel from the pavement over
And over again and the sound dims in the distance
Tires sink into potholes making sounds like
The beat of a base drum keeping time
An ice cream truck bell rings a metallic allure
A voice calls out from across the street
Like Charlie Rouse on Boo Boo's Birthday

The traffic-light is a maestro who orchestrates but
With two commands
Red and Green/Stop and Go

To hear all these sounds is to be in the moment
To value these sounds is to be consciously
Linked to the cosmos
To transfer them into another genre
Deepens their aesthetics
Acquiring this ability takes a prodigious artist

THE RECONSTRUCTION

With a blank music sheet versed in a great art
Monk stomp his foot to the pavement
And throw out his arms as antennas
To take in the sounds

He recognizes the hesitation between the lyrical clamors
And it's expected monotonous cadenced
He smiles at the missing beat and he owns it
He hears the nimble tinkle of sounds that make harmony
With their huskier relatives after bypassing
The notes that are in their natural progression
And he adopts it and adept it into a technique
Of off beats and silence and decisive hesitancy
He combines this new discovery with hip idioms he
Had mastered from the past in Straight no Chaser
He finds his route maneuvering in heavy traffic

Monk pulls in his antennas
Regains a walking stance
Cover his delicate fingers with gray gloves
And reaching Sixty-Fourth Street
He turns the corner

Now he composes with an original ear a billboard
Of pioneering musical enchantments shaped from the
Sounds of life in the unseen spaces on Amsterdam Avenue.

A Different Point of View

Snapshots

It is strange the things one does
When there is nothing to do.
I drove the back dirt roads
Of a neighboring county making
So many turns I was uncertain
I would later find my way back.
Arousing my descriptive instincts
Making verbal snapshots of what I saw.

Snapshot:
The sun hung brightly in the noon position.
Angel shaped clouds decorated the blue sky.
The land full with corn green and high
On either side of the road.
The fields rolled by healthy and unending.
I could feel God smiling on these acres.

Snapshot:
Ahead the road circled an old mushroom shaped
Moss filled tree and returned to itself
Under the tree an obscure figure
The road circled between the tree and a wooden
Framed house with a tin roof and a porch
That wrapped around the house.

Snapshot:
Below the tree on a wooden chair sat a man.
His face was worn wrinkled tan leather.
Huge bags hung under weak gray watery eyes.
He wore overalls and a green tee shirt.
His right bony arm was made of veins.
His left arm was missing from the elbow.
He was seventy-five, or maybe a hundred years old.

Howdy, trying to find the paved road, I said.
He sized me up in silence, never once looked at me.
He didn't make a motion nor spoke a word.
Mysteriously, he summoned me from the truck.
I joined the engulfing silence under the tree.

I once had to kill a man, he said
His watery eyes finally merging into mine.
I felt a chill dance down my back.

I once had to kill a man,
Cause he didn't leave me a choice.
I was cutting firewood for supper
That evening he marched up here
Plunder on his mind and in his heart.
Making demands, he had no rights too.
My wife, her soul gone to rest
And my young children all grown
And moved off north now
Bounded to the crops of this land
Labored five years and never seen
More than some sacks of rice
And grits and some salted fat meat.
He had long seized my dignity
Now he wanted to own my manhood.

He ain't never broke a sweat
And he lived in a fine big house.
Although it was his land my family
More than mere tenets he could work
And be rid of with a wave of his hand.
Sure it was his seeds and his mule
And his plow – but it was my sweat that
Built his fine big house and put beef on
His table and I known it.

His voice grew mean and threatening.
His words turned ugly and dangerous.
His face red and frightful.
His body shook as he stomped the ground.
He wanted me and my family gone.
Then he made his move.

I can't say how it all happened.
I had the wood ax in my hand
When things turned black
And the wind came hurling from the fields
And the lightning bolts shot 'cross the heavens.
Thunder roared in the sky
Shaking the earth under my feet.
I felt rain on my face
I felt rain on my chest
I felt rain on my ax hand
I looked and I saw the rain was red
I looked and I saw the wet was blood.
The wind went away innocently
The lightening creased without taint
The thunder hushed without guilt
And I buried him under the house yonder
And of this deed
Not ever a whisper 'til now.

The old man looked down at the ground
His spell over me broken
I ran back to the truck feeling unlucky
And laden with what I'd heard.

I drove fast over those dirt roads
As the sun hung low over the fields.

A Different Point of View

Snapshot:
An old abandoned house
Wooden and weather beaten
Half stood by the road
Its roof collapsed under
The weight of time and neglect
A ghost of another era
Now a haven for reptiles.

Up ahead a caution sign
I was approaching an intersection
Offering choices
And there it was – the paved road
I made the right turn and drove.

Snapshot:
An old country store dressed in all
The signs of the past stood behind
Antiquated gas pumps.
An old pickup truck parked to the side
Three soda crates lined the earthen entranceway.
My thirst led me to stop.

Snapshot:
A large man with a pumpkin face
Tomato cheeks and sandy hair
Sat half hidden behind two candy canisters
On the counter in a corner of the store
His body and spirit linked to this scene.

I drank a soda in this quaint place
Charmingly ancient with a southern inclination
Pleasing to one sense of history
While abhorrent to another
An expression of what went wrong
For the man under the tree.

A Note from the Future

Time is the measured border between
The events of history
It happened framed in that time
Like time travelers, some events of history
Jump measured borders to echo itself
In other blocks of time.

I become disoriented by the discussion
Concerning a confederate flag
Flying atop a statehouse
Migrating events and sentiments of another century
Recast to scramble my sense of this time
And the chilly winds of the past are again.

A black boy is tied to
A tree beaten and terrorized
An event that jumbled my time compass
And my senses stumbled about like
A drunken politician in the darkness
Assaulting the depository of truth.
And I cry out: What century is this?

A little black girl's face
Is used for a note pad
A modern method more futuristic
Than the sticky pad which comes
With the warning: Test before using
This is a note from the future
History travels in all directions.

For some events of history
The past is also the present
And sometimes also the future.

A Different Point of View

A museum to resurrect the history
Of hooded hoods is all
The testimony this point needs
A home for the past here in the present
Glorifying the misdeeds of subversives and
Bigots, hooded and bare face, past and present
In nostalgic longings to break the shackles
Of measured time bygone to arrive in the future

For some events of history
The past is also the present
And sometimes also the future.

Some Old Men

Some old men know the autumn by
The frailty of limb and bone
Some by the loss of appetite
Or the long sleepless nights.

Some old men reshape the past in
Their minds/what could have been
Some work hard at altering the
Course/directing the *now*.

Some old men measure the worth of their
Lives by the size of the kingdom accumulated
Some by the wealth of good service rendered
And the growth of their hearts.

Some old men stay young with
Enthusiasm for work, family, idealism
And take joy from life
But truly old is the man who
Gauges his quality of life
By the empty youthfulness of
The woman at his breakfast table.

Oh Years How You Do

For Uncle Leaser

Oh years how you do
Even to a good man
A man of the sun who
Was himself not perfect
But a guiding light for
Family, friends and community.

Oh years who balances your
Scales of good and evil – who
Writes the names of those who
Should escape the wrath of time
By a gentle retreat into eternity.

Is it that your plan
Is no plan and your wheel
Is random
And life and
Uncle Leaser's affliction
Is like the lotto/
You got to be in it to win it.

Legacy

For Fannie Lou Hamer

Born just a short distance from bondage time
Into a life of servitude, deprivation and bigotry
The daughter of a sharecropper
The wife of a sharecropper
There appeared no way out
This was all there was going to be
Not even the faintest glimmer of hope

Born with God's gift of courage and a sense
Of self that would not be subjugated by any other
She was a human woman being who
One day discovered the vote and the power it held
For this she was kicked off the plantation
And into a life of gallantry where her singing stiffened
Backs and inspired resolve in a cowered people

They sent her from her home, they threatened her
They shot at her, they followed her around
They beat her like she was a man – near blind
Her mission and her song came from On-high
Such enduring courage they had never encountered
As with this woman who came to right ancient wrongs
And would not be denied the vote for us all

She made her mark testifying at the Democratic
National Convention in New Jersey, in 1964
She became a national spearhead to win the vote
Her leadership abilities organized people to a cause
She built consequential institutions that helped
Bring dignity, power, hope and the vote to us all
Her remains in Ruleville, MS, her spirit roams the
Nation, her soul rest in eternity.

Gratitude
For Rene Davidson

Take this thank you note I send
For believing you should help me
And for trying to and thinking you
Owed me because I was kind to Debbie

I think you came to like me not
Merely because it was fashionable
To right some ancient wrongs
You were astonished by my durability
And my audacity to think myself
Worthy so you thought me worthy too

Through the strength of my friendship
With daughter Debbie I have become
Allied with the Davidson clan –

Isaac Singer says there are
No falsehoods
All things are true to some degree.

A Different Point of View

Lupin Proletariat was all we were -
Capitalist pig, brutal whitey, stinking honky
Bourgeoisie, bloodsucker, control freak
Is how I once learned to express my displeasure
Of the oppression you heaped upon me
And my kin and my kind.

I saw you as the thing you done to me
And I understood what you done to me
Done for you
And your kin and your kind.

Martin Luther King Jr. understood it.

Under the guise of securing my rights
He set out to make you a better human being
To change your evil ways
To rouse you from your insanity.

And finally you lay the tyranny down
I hold out my hand and now
As you advance towards that prospect
Of you
I come towards a different point of view.

The Reconstruction

She was black -
Her dress was black
Her aura was black
A familiar blackness
An all knowing blackness
Everything about her was that
Blackness which provokes awakening.

She flew in from the East
Her destination was all-encompassing
Every heart and every soul
And from her eyes an inborn
Truth scattered
Her smile was love - shared
And her voice roars like a teardrop.

We stood there in silent and complete
Submission
To the axiom of the Universal
Host
Our hearts merged to one
As we sailed to a new and different
Harbor
The words of our souls
Became a song of a
Sameness.

And the reach of her supremacy
Covered the earth
And all the galaxies
As we sailed to a peace and
Oneness.

And it is on the wings
Of this spirit -
We shall *all* have arrived.

The Insurrection

Sing it Out

The arts are rising again here
In the hearts of a people entrapped
Sing it out

Sacred dark enchanters
Are being reborn
Here in Babylon

Pharaoh's horn sounds new life
He was the son in the trinity of free-form jazz
Baraka's pen points the way
In and out of Spirit House
Otto Neals paints oases highlighting
The artists of the Weusi Art Collective

Sing it out
The Arts are rising again

Through the arts into reality
From reality into the arts
Blackness forges into its true form
And shape lives
And shape minds
And make the spirit sing
The arts are rising again.

The White Man is the Devil

He has raped and plundered all
My people from our homeland
To the fields of America
Lynched and whipped us shattered our
Humanity disrupt our ability to communicate
With each other in our native tongue
Put his dogs upon us

Soil our women, shackled our men
Sold our children fettered our spirits
Kept us like livestock

Never can this beast convert from
His evil past no generation of his breed
Can ever erase his criminality
It is indeed his lot to be
The thing that God forever frowns upon

The thing the Nation of Islam
Knows he to be
The white man is the devil itself.

The Middle Passage

Let us know my brothers and sisters, the anguished cry
Of a people shocked into a haunting silence by
The mystery of their looming destiny captured and tied;
Marched to Elmina Castle chained, dehumanized together
Shackled and counted there
They are stunned by the nightmare
Of the dark chambers and the cold dungeon floor

They are assembled there; Fulani, Edo, Yoruba, Hausa
Ashanti, Ewe, Basaa, Mende – people of the African Coast
All of a different tongue and a same karma that now
Awakens natural spirits of cyclonic winds and torrential rains
To follow them into this deepest unknown of the
Atlantic Ocean, forever - year upon year upon year

They are forced through the Door of No Return
Chained to the creaking hulk of an oak built vessel
Iron neck collars, chained hands and chained feet they
Are stacked indiscriminately like common freight in that
Damp dark hole of filth, disease and the stench of death
Bewilderment and a communal wail of anguish their only
Response; their only common possessions

For many the journey ends at the bottom of the ocean
They go over when their strength can carry them no more
They go over when they aggressively protest their situation
They go over when water and rations cannot sustain them all
They go over of their own accord from the fear that these
beast
Will eat them on another land or they will sail off the edge of
earth

Let us know my brothers and sisters that the firmaments
Turned the sound of their lamentation into a twirling
whirlwind
And the sea into an angry tropical typhoon matching the
outrage
Of the enslavers as this breach in human nature is so
abnormally
Horrific and brutal Cosmic Divinity is offended by this
ruthless
Betrayal of man and God angry whirlwind are generated by
The spirits at the bottom of the sea forever an
Encoded reminder marking the route of the slaughter

Look around you my brothers and sisters to witness
The miracle we all are; remember from where we come
Descendants of the survivors of the horrors
Of the Middle Passage
We have come through the distance of geography
We have come through the distance of time
We have come through the distance of culture
To know the anguish of those who command the ocean.

The Insurrection

For Fred Hampton

I am not crazy, nor mad or insane
Still I must die this death to vindicate my humanity
Within myself there is harmony
Still the antagonism on my outer world
Has drawn me to this suicide
When they come I will fight
Why else have I come this course but
To have the world recognize that
I have for too long been maligned

I know who and what I am
And there is peace
Yet there remains the compulsion
To have the world concede
My calamity and suppress this affliction
When they come I will fight
Even when their awakening comes
By-way of my death

I take up arms as a martyr
For the future of my son's son
And his son's son.
That they will live free
In America and know
A genuine American Justice
When they come I will fight.

My Thing

You can not hinder
My progress
Life's directions
My own to decide.

Damn your means
Of control
Confound you.

I have arrived within myself –
Liberated.

The History of New Music in America (9)

The first Africans upon the slave ships destined
For the America's sensed the coming of
A great and lasting catastrophe
They had nothing that would
Protect and fortify them
From the coming centuries of bondage and tyranny
So they sent out an exalting wail
Beseeching God's mercy
God looked down on them and saw
That they had nothing
They were naked and in chains
God in His singular wisdom
Took the very sound of their lament
And turned it into their shield and their weapon
And today we call that sound music
It is those majestic wails
Those cries of despair
That music
In its ever changing forms
From field holler to hip-hop
That has nourished our spirits through the centuries
A sound that spoke directly to On-high
For sustenance to keep the spirit
Unyielding to the horrors of shackled burdens
Feeble and conquered, music
Became our sacred shield
And our consecrated weapon.

Welfare

Why is Whitey
Crying about one
Out of every eight
New Yorkers
Being on relief?
…Shit
He's most of the
Seven that's working.

The Tiger and the Cat

For Bernice Miller & Ima Cobb
(Two White Teachers I Know)

The tiger wants the ideas
That travel within the written word
To tear at the skin – to draw blood
To convince and conquer
To claw the inner eye to a reality
Of our choice – make the world
To our image
She is relentless.

The cat purrs at the inner workings
Of the mind, heart and soul
Trying to understand – or explain
What impels us to love or hatred
To war or work – to invent or destroy
She wants us to comprehend
Who we are and what we are
And why -
She is relentless.

Because of the tiger and the cat
In all these pursuits
I am relentless.

A Different Point of View

One Woman
For Nina Simone

It was 1957 I heard you sing
About loving Porgy your voice
Claiming the love and anguish
Of our striving tribe
I fell instantly in love with
Your voice, your music and you.

I said hello to you on Lenox Avenue
I cherished your concerts from
Front row seats.

I closed my eyes and wandered
Through your defiant rejection
Of humiliation and injustice
Your passionate rendition of
The songs of our traditions
You stretched creative arrangements
To take a great music to higher levels
And I heard in your voice – my voice

The sun's gonna shine in
My back door backdoor
Someday.

Ten Mark Annie

The black opal, sleek, clean and erotic
As a stealth lover
Makes its quiet night run on Nuremberg Street
Those first nights after the eagle has flown
And young soldiers eager for escape
And carnal fantasies crowd the narrow street

The driver a business woman, a vendor
Of lost moment and pleasures
Capable of the magic that briefly
Nullifies loneliness
Points a finger to the next sojourner
From the solitude of a foreign land
While the others wait with eager anticipation

Annie Gunther an old woman in her thirties
Lay her blanket in the German forests
A short distance outside the city
And goes directly to work
The drive out to the woods was itself foreplay
In short the opal is back on Nuremberg Street
To collect the next set of brown bones.

Yesterday's Poets

Each noon by a little hut
At the base of a small hill
Where nearby a stream ebbed
Gently from the city –
Sat a poet
Humbly feasting on charitable nourishment
After he was finished
He offered a prayer for his benefactors
And folded his legs
To contemplate the states of affairs -
Sadly
The poet had not lived among the people
So how was he to know?

Christianity

The Northern clergy
Busloads went South
Days when dogs were biting
Water hoses slung children for yards
Not one nightstick stayed still –
They went south giving
Fortitude
To those being brutalized.

At which I have often wondered
Is this the role for the church?
Should they have not
Gone to the oppressors
Grab up a cracker a piece
Throw them to their knees
And baptize them in Christianity?

THE INSURRECTION

For Benjamin Moloise

*"As you have had to bury our children today
so shall the blood of these heroes be avenged."*

Winnie Mandela-

From where in the universe and
How did these breasts reach earth
With glutton gut and
Swollen voracious jowls and
Ugly instincts
These so-called Afrikaners who say
They have no other place to live
(The deal being they are marooned on earth.)

Some say they are descendants
Of the worse 17th century Europeans
That torments humanity with such beastliness
Of violent twisted logic and pretentious indignation
As these Afrikaners
Who chain the body and aspiration of a people
These beast who
Lashed, pummeled, mauled and hammered
The body of a prince to eternal rest
Hold a king captive decade upon decade
Fearing deadly his freedom
Forced you – the poet – to walk to the gallows
Gallantly singing your freedom poem
Sent aimed bullets into the bodies
Of children innocent yet of any
Intent to harm the beast.

Where in the universe could
Such things exist before their
Arrival here on a planet
Already burdened with human cruelty

A Different Point of View

And how long will be their stay
These so-called Afrikaners who lie
About not having elsewhere to go
Still one day they will be shown the
Direction back to their own hell.

To Steve Biko

The sky turned dark
And the sea was black
And the streets were dark black
And the storm was swift and sure.

The children needed freedom
A poet sang the song of ANC
Freedom from the gallows
The father of freedom's needs
Entered a third decade imprisoned.

Enough
Rage
The tides turned
ANC.

And the sky turned blue
And the clouds were the only white
And the sea ran free
And the streets were clean
And the bush was green
And all remembered your name.

A Different Point of View

And He Was Pretty Too

He was a whiz fist blur fast
He could run, never needed to hide
He had goals; he had skill, he had power
He had heart, he had word, and he had integrity
He was the people's cherished champion
He was the greatest and he was pretty too.

Long lean legs, tasseled white shoes
Danced the prologue to the night's intrigue
One question abound -
In which round
Will the people's opponent go down?
Like Langston's longhead jazz players
Ali improvised as he worked as he entertained
Ali was Bird, Diz, Monk, Miles
Be-bop bip-bop be-bop rope-a-dope.

A mere boxer as things go, Ali
Embodied the aspirations of a people
The essence of a time, the gist of an era
In his fist, in his words, in his deeds
Ali became our symbol of defiance.

His playfulness helped us to laugh
Through our pains
His courage inspired us onward
His success gave us hope for ourselves.

For all of this we adore him
For all of this we canonize him
For all of this we love him
Muhammad Ali is the greatest
And he is pretty too.

Thelonious Sphere Monk

I was floored when Charlie Rico
Brought him to my room (in my mother's house)
I played a recording he made with
The 'Trane
He pranced to the beat
And recreated his riff
Only one of five jazzmen
To grace the cover of Time
Magazine pioneer in be-bop
We spoke then they left.

Monk was exceptional in many things
Math, physics and Ping-Pong and
It's cool that he referred to himself as
The-onlyest Monk

Monk rose from Minton's Playhouse
'Round Midnight
Using silence and hesitation
In a style never heard before
Made them go Straight No Chaser
I remembered our conversation
Then
In Walked Bud.

Coltrane Talks to God

Let me introduce the players:
Miles Davis on trumpet
John Coltrane on saxophone
Wynton Kelly on piano
Paul Chambers on bass and
Billy Cobb on drums

Teo

Da dum tum/da dum tum/da dum tum

After a few bars of a thumping bass introduction
The rhythm section joins in for a few bars more
Before Miles begins the sacrament with a calm call
Evoking flourishes from the ensemble that slowly evolves
Into a delightful bounce of notes that dance with
Themselves enchanted and charmed
Each by the other

Energy, the flow of energy and the spirit are summoned
Ultimate realities the All of All that is - the sameness
All distinctions are relative comparisons
We now will hear the shapes and the forms
Which cannot be expressed in words
The only contrast to what is unknown
Nonetheless instinctively adhered to

Miles blow a series of sharp notes
That jolts the atmosphere and repeats
Again and again in sight variations
Developing into the resolve of the hymn
Of preparation for the sermon – all the while
The rhythm section is keeping up a driving orderliness
While Miles elaborates an unobtrusive passion like

A Different Point of View

The energy that amassed before the big bang
And rolls out the expansion of the universe
For now this orderliness exist to contain
Within its perimeter what's to come

A piano interlude builds to reaffirm
The primacy of orderliness before
Coltrane burst into consciousness

And then it happens
Coltrane enters like cleansing rain
Thunder and lightning illuminating
Abandon streets on a dark Harlem night
A gathering for all concerned coalitions
Echoes of the turmoil of the times coalesce
The emotion builds and become intricate, convoluted
And twist over and over again and changes into
Repeated screams – dark and chaotic
Turbulent images bubble within framed orderliness
Coltrane makes repeated calls gathering all complexities
Then he beseechs in a new language of shapes and forms
Chaotic precision an oxymoron regarding quantum
mechanics
The Theory of Everything –
Particles of sub-atomic sounds beseeching
Beseeching earnestly beseeching

This has been a voyage to awareness

Coltrane is disengaging from the unpredictable
Turbulence of sub-atomic particles
And glides up to relativity earthly realities
Where Miles can handle the transfer though
He is exhausted from the energy spent
Translating the logic of Coltrane's sermon
In a few tones he regains the confidence of his

THE INSURRECTION

Own instincts which are born anew from
The Coltrane performance – we are all one now
Miles sounds his last note -
Understanding in at the core of every quest
The rhythm section alone closed the curtains.

To George Jackson

"Alright gentlemen, I'm taking over now."

Jonathan Jackson-

Warrior, revolutionary, Soledad brother
Spirit of that which is truly free
You have shown the world that
A certain inner freedom is possible
Although the body is imprisoned
And life uncertain
Isolated and beaten.

You kept the faith
Kept your thoughts on freedom
Kept your mind free
And the other things didn't matter.

It is a shining lesson you
Have left to those of us
Body free/imprisoned mind.

An Old Couple on the Subway

He looked in his late sixties
Beaten gray and senseless
By the years –
A king born without a throne
Or the time to resurrect one
He sat playing a silly game.

Her age about the same
She sat exasperated
By his silly game
But displayed the dignity
Of a queen
Whose king was born
Without a throne
Just dreams and fallacies.

Green Haven in Autumn

"...and all I can say is thank God for penitentiaries."
Richard Pryor-

Green Haven has a wall
High, gray, and I take it
With insanity locked inside
Its secured cement dormitories.

I surveyed the land as my friend
When in to visit his brother.

The surrounding grounds
Is fall in October
Falling leaves of
Pretty autumn colors
On hills of every hue
That makes the wall
Should want to crumble.

The wall looks impregnable
To nature's warm sentiment
Or my dreamy vision of
The landscape
It looks of the worst gray weather
And feels not a tender smile
Or the pretty autumn colors
That makes the wall
Should want to crumble.

Irony

The Fallacy of
The American Dream
Composed by zealots
Nurtured by bigots
Vintage in the violence
In which it was born.

Gossip

What's that you say?
        Say what again?
I hear you
    You don't say
I'm all ears
      Run it
Say what again?
        Who?
Oh yeah
  With who?
Who else?
    Man, you can't mean...
No shit
  Now ain't that a bitch
You know me
  I ain't heard a thing.

.

Untitled Statement #1 in Haiku

There is no
Such thing
As war

Just
Madmen
Eating

At the flesh
Of
God.

Post Card from Viet Nam 1968

My country tis of thee
Sweet land of liberty
Of thee I sing

Here I am in Viet Nam
Learning a new trade
Smoking dope and hunting down
Primitive thinking people

Trying to survive and if I do

When I get back to America
I'm not gonna give up my new trade
Of smoking dope and hunting down
Primitive thinking people

My country tis of thee
Sweet land of liberty
Of thee I sing.

An Obscene Poem

All the elements were forming to set the national tone
Anti-war protesters/civil rights marchers/
Counter-culture creatures smoking dope in the streets
Engaged and enraged to challenge the monolith:
The Silent Moral Majority
Judged to be neither silent nor moral.

The countryside polarized
The cities polarized
The nation polarized
The majesty that is the unrealized
Ideal of America lost its foundation
In a lawless presidency
The course was set.

Soon rotating her firm funky bottom
Down that flaw section of democracy row
America the tempest
Innocent and sweet as her ideal
Treacherous and oppressive as her reality.

The rapist stalked the Watergate Hotel
America's virtue was assaulted the veil
Of her promises ripped from her frame
She offered scant resistance her legs
Where a people's freedom dwell
Were easily opened.

I became aroused watching
Nixon do it to America
As she twisted and turned
Squirmed and screamed
Moaning softly
Ooh police, ooh impeach

A Different Point of View

Ooh police, ooh impeach
All the while truly enjoying
The perverted positions of a
Tricky dick
Nixon.

The Pipers

In indifference their song
Is sung from within
While in slumber
Throughout their souls
Cry out a jubilant dying melody
Destine to walk the earth
Scorned and shrouded
The looters and the victims
Their plight serves the slurs
Of politician's rhetoric.

And try you;
Reach out to them a hand to help
They shall certainly not recognize
Neither care nor concern
The lure is formidable
The fog is blinding
They will sham you
Then laugh at you in the quiet
Of their death march.

Singing souls of a mournful tune
With a compulsion that caters to
Only the present urgency
Hearts attuned to their souls singing
A pitiful song
Yet has not the power to humble them
As their present needs are the greater
And their lives are lived in unmarked graves.

The Witness

It all happened quite suddenly
Man's fury turned against him
The air became dense
The sky mushroomed
The flowers wilted and died
…I stood the only witness.

Death raged
Death raged like an angry beast
And hope proved to be death by radiation
The human will is dispirited
City dwellers crawled into the streets to die
People died however they could
People killed themselves
And murdered each other
And with the world in the midst
Of all this madness
Willie across the street
Screwed himself to death.

No longer were there trees
Building crumbled/the rivers dried
And when all things were dead
There standing for a witness
Stood I.

Now all living things cease to be
There was never a baby born
And Jesus didn't died on the cross
If I forget
The poet's lyrics never sweetened the air
And all of man's majesty
None of it is real
Ain't none this stuff real without a witness.

Panhandler's Message

Roaming nights running, running
Searching for whatever falls
Through the safety net
Day be coming soon
I nod then wake waiting
The warmth of day
And the invasion of your world
Upon mine.

You carry the deed
But the world is mine
I am home where it is I be
I don't visit you, rather
You visit me.

My life is entrusted with the wind
I would never make a commitment to you
For then I would have to suffer your authority
And leave my home forty hours a week.

Death on 64ᵗʰ Street

With a history assorted as the world's great boulevards
But little known, never celebrated and seldom heralded
A thoroughfare that once led to Death Avenue
Where the trolleys and freight trains crushed
Reckless boys and girls seeking adventure
In the trains yards of West End Avenue.

Where neighbors bartered goods and services
And peddlers dumped dreams and premonitions
Boys played stickball in between motor traffic
Wives carried provisions up steeped tenement flights
The daily parade of the baby carriages
Brought new life to the street.

Where landlords gouged tenants in Coldwater Flats
And Saturday night instituted fights and recriminations
Bootleggers kept credit accounts
And number bankers operated on a cash only basis
A block so old with custom and remnants of the past
Live chickens were sold at Katz Poultry Shack.

Where Saturdays brought the confluent of a village square
In a ghetto community rich with relationships
But known for its snarled feuds – tribal and personal
Sunday promenades returning from church well dressed
A third of the street gave way to change in 1947
Otherwise change was something that happened elsewhere

Where this Saturday morning a grudge had to be settled
A tall dark well-dressed man waited patiently
Near the glass window of the Century Bar
Soon as he saw his transgressor
He flung open the door
The partly hidden knife gleaming from sunlight

THE INSURRECTION

He called out the man's name
His intentions and a dirty word –
Said he was making good on his promise
To kill him and he plunged the knife downward
Towards the pavement of 64th Street.

Numbers Player

Honey, I just got to play
My numbers – you know
It's like having a full stomach
My dreams of hitting big.

People get carried off
On all kinds of distractions
Some people use dope, some drink
Some play around – you know
I don't knock anyone for their habits
I just like to play my numbers
Like having a full stomach
When my 058 is in and
All them dreams are ready to jump out at me.

The other day I had to go to the hospital
Where they informed me I had to stay
For a few days
I stole the time to get my figures in
058 and 125 and 652 and 919 and 347
Even before they put me in a room
I had to get my digits in -
Numbers is my habit
Not like dope, booze or success
But satisfies my dreams just the same.

Talking To You

When it's difficult to talk to you
I talk to the plants
Long intricate conversations about
Love, family finances, world politics
The New York Knicks.

Plants understand and have emotions
And they listen and respond
So when it's difficult to talk with you
I sit down with the geranium, the weeping fig
The gardenia, the Jade plant
And have my say.

But I'm careful what I say
What tone of voice
And choice of words is very
Important to a plant's response
A kind and gentle word promotes
Their growth.

Last week when it was difficult to talk
With you and you said those words
You know what words – out loud
In front of the plants and
Our cissus rhombifolia committed suicide
It was because of that tone – and that voice.

Plants have emotions and they respond
So you ought not to talk to me that way
In front of the plants.

Of Man and Nature

I like best
Those things that
Were here
Before man started
Building.

I like the open sky
That will not lie
Not these city building
Scraping the sky with
Lies and lies and lies.

A New York City Eviction
(Remembering the last day in the life of Eleanor Bumpurs)

98 dollars in arrears to the New York City
Housing Authority – her rent was due
The accountant in the rent office following
Procedure filed an eviction notice on an old woman
Having trouble with her health and her reality
And unable to manage her affairs of the moment

Her psychosis intensified during the Reagan presidency
When evil seeped through her walls with an harassing
High pitched shrill and left feces in her bath tub
Her assigned social workers were uninterested
To get her the help she so desperately needed
To be institutionalized away from the real evil
Soon coming to do her lethal bodily harm

The eviction task was passed down to a police assault team
Armed with gladiator shields and a Y shaped restraining bar
And clubs and 12 gauge shotguns – eviction?

(I once saw a b&w movie; the cops were Pat O'Brian
George Raft, Edmond O'Brien and Reagan/the actor
In a similar situation widow Mary O'Malley behind on her
Rent was about to be evicted – the cops in the squadron
Passed the hat to raise the *dough* to pay the widow's rent
Doing anything else would have been solely frowned upon
Plus these men had to go on living with themselves)

In this modern day Technicolor version of the same story
The thought of philanthropy never crossed their minds
No one from the rent office to the police squadron
Could entertain a generous gesture nor a humane offer

A Different Point of View

They drilled out her door knob to peep through the hole
And saw her naked and frightened her one human instinct
To protect herself with a kitchen knife from well-armed
Evil pounding down her door in an organized assault
There could be no escape she met them head-on
They tried clumsily to pin her to the wall with the Y shape
bar
A cop who was not an O'Brien, a Raft or a Reagan/the
actor
But a Sullivan let loose a blast from the 12 gauge that
Nearly took off her hand welding the kitchen knife and in an
Instant later another blast to her chest served the eviction
notice.

Blues

Blues is a fine
Sister
Four feet tall
Blues is a Monday morning
And that ain't all
Blues is nothing
When it's in your pocket
And your stomach
Blues is a workweek
That lasts so long
Blues is a paycheck
That's gotten, then gone
Blues is a sweet song
Some of the time
Blues is that little
Black gal of mine.

Soul Food

For Lewis H. Michaux

Been out there all day
In a world that's cold
Then
Go home to
Enjoy some soul.

I grabbed a good book
Kissed a pretty cook
And nestled close to the radiator.

The rice was on
And had begun to boil
Why there was cornbread
In the oven – and all.

Now to bring this meal
Down to earth
There was cooked
Greens and ox tails
Washed of their dirt.

When the meal was eaten
And all the world's wrongs
Were temporally righted
I kissed the cook
Read the book and
Out the window took a look
Tomorrow again I'll face
That world that's cold.

Salvation

I was born into this quandary
As so many of us are
This was not in the beginning
A situation of my own construction
But hear this not as a complaint
Or a hollow holler.

Strife and hardship is what I've known
Still I go on
Disappointment and disillusionment
Has been my fare
Still I go on
Knowing full well that up ahead
Plain as the mind's eye can see
There is a clearing in the woods
A clearing in the woods for me.

Revolution

Swinging night sticks
Rabid dogs
The hangman noose
And bombed black girls
Didn't start a revolution.

Malcolm and King's dead
Rap's been taken off...somewhere?
Roy Wilkins sings the blues off key
And even that won't start a revolution
Though
There is talk of one coming.

Most folk said it came
When Sammy Davis chucked his process
For an Afro
But even that didn't start a revolution.

The filth of neglected streets
Apartments without heat
And I know rats
By their first names
Our babies die eating paint from the wall
Some overdose in their kindergarten class
And if the police were to shoot you
And your Momma dead
That wouldn't start a revolution
Though
There is talk of one coming.

Ras the Exhorter

Listen brothers and sisters
To the mournful cry of a people
Being led to the dock of defeat and despair
Herded onto the ships of bondage
While the past severed in a night
Red of fire
And the fortunate died
Clinging to the bosom of Mother Africa
And upon the blooded shore
Laid a child drowned
While in search of its mother
Who at that very instant
(Upon a vessel destined for America)
Sang...the first song of terror
The first song of sorrow
The first song of shame and survival
The first Blues.

Listen brothers and sisters
To the spirit of that child
As it whispers in the wind
The rumors of rebellion
To an African who had not yet lost himself
And who upon hearing these rumors
Died in Mutiny
And the many passively buried him
Deafened by the sound of
Whispered rumors in the wind
A people withered in the fields
For a second and a third century
But only those who heard the whispered
Rumors of a child in search
Lived a death of defiance.

THE INSURRECTION

Brothers and sisters
A child has not seen its mother
For three hundred years and
Longs to hold her near
And still he whispers
In the wind the rumors of liberation
And when we too hear
The whispered rumors in the wind
The search of a child shall be over.

Harlem

You ever been to Harlem/river to river/old Harlem
Harlem cradle of a new migration of beleaguered seekers
Harlem of wide boulevards and crowded streets
Speakeasy Harlem embracing jazz sounds and
Blues people arriving North from Southern
Cotton fields and Midwestern honky-tonks
Harlem of Marcus Garvey Universal Negro
Harlem of the New Negro Movement/135 Street
Center of the Black Capital of thought/Harlem
Renaissance in music/literature/letters and arts

You ever been to Harlem/World War II/Harlem
Of Army browns and melancholy waves goodbye
Of zoot suited happy feet stomping at the Savoy
Of jolly crowds at rent parties peddling pickled pig's feet
Harlem of Father Divine and Sweet Daddy Grace
A charitable Harlem/an acquiring Harlem
Harlem of the Lafayette Theater and Joe Louis
Culture and power on the ascend/ numbers runners
Brandishing hopes and dreams on a ten cent play
Lewis Michaux's African Memorial Bookstore
The house of common sense and proper propaganda
This prideful Harlem sent Adam Clayton Powell, Jr
To Congress in 1944 to keep the faith, baby

You ever been to Harlem/Jackie Robinson/Harlem
Where in 1947 little boys inspired to hit that stick-ball
A little bit further to reach their personal Ebbits Field
Harlem where things were not quite equal but peaches
And cream in comparison to from where they came
Harlem home of Ralph Ellison's novel/Invisible Man
Harlem where Queen Mother Moore is rediscovered
Harlem/Gillespie/Parker/Monk were the first Beboppers

THE INSURRECTION

You ever been to Harlem/ sixties militant/ Harlem
Harlem where Malcolm X preached Black Liberation
Harlem/Amiri Baraka/ stirred the Black Arts Movement
The Last Poets in the East / Apollo Theater in the West
None too far in distance and ideology from Una Mulzac's
Ark of knowledge /Liberation Bookstore
If you don't know/learn/If you know/ teach/she advocated
Harlem/Mother Hale ordained compassion at Hale House
Harlem/illuminating a bond to Mother Africa from its core
A healing home coming for Middle Passage survivors
You ever been to Harlem/Down Boys/Harlem
Shady deals of Nicky Barnes and Frank Lucas
Harlem gangsters doing the work of the tyrants preceding
The three horsemen of Harlem/ crack/graffiti/hip hop
Harlem of the crystal vial crack one pull you're whacked
That also was Harlem for far too long a decade or two
Harlem/Graffiti insisted and won some respect once it
Went from the streets and the trains/moved to art galleries
Hip hop though Bronx born/symbolized the better known
Harlem/which drove it to the top of American culture

You ever been to Harlem/familiar/routine/Harlem
Pork chops and ribs/fish and chips/chicken and waffles
Liqueur stores and halleluiah temples and movie theaters
Co-exist serving the same patrons in separate locations
Amongst infinitely inviting features /river to river Harlem
Lenox Avenue/Mount Morris Park/Sugar Hill/1-2-5- Street
When Harlem calls/come to Harlem
Not to change its charm/but to join it/be of it
One day you'll want to come to Harlem and live
There too and be a proud juncture in its history

You ever been to Harlem?

Acknowledgements

Bill Chatman, My Friend
Thelonious Sphere Monk
64th Street: Poetic Portrait: The African People of San Juan
Hill, Horace Mungin Books, 2011

Nourishment
Syncopation
Salvation: A Millennial Sampler of South Carolina Poetry,
Ninety-Six Press, 2005

And He Was Pretty Too
The Union Man
Nourishment: 365 Degrees, The Point Newspaper,
winter, 2001

Juba Zula
The Witness
Talking to You: The Ninety-Six Sampler of South Carolina
Poetry, Ninety-Six Press, 1994

To Steve Biko: New Rain, Volume Six, Blind Beggar Press,
1986

Welfare: Nommo, The Macmillan Company, 1972

Of Man and Nature
Blues: Black Out Loud, The Macmillan Company, 1970

My Thing: The New York Times, April 25, 1969

Blues
Untitled Statement # 1 in Haiku
Harlem
Welfare: Now See Here, Homes, Brothers Publication, 1969

Irony
My Thing
Of Man and Nature
Soul Food: Dope Hustler's Jazz, Brothers Publication, 1968

Here's what's been said about the author and his work over the years.

The poem "My Thing" by Horace Mungin deals with a major theme of the black revolution that is frequently expressed in cries for "liberation," for self-determination and for a positive identity. It is in this way characteristic of much of the poetry written today (1969) by young black Americans, a part of a renaissance of arts, letters, music and drama." **Thomas Johnson, The New York Times.**

Before this too-long, cold month is over, we want to thank you for your (1971) reading…your terse, sharp insights stay with us, and we've grateful for your sharing of experience and perceptions. **Ruth Van Doren, New School for Social Research.**

Irony is the weapon of the powerless, and as they say in the joint… (1991), author Mungin, who has been around for a while, since the time of the swell of the 60's Black Arts Movement is laying on symbol, very heavy, but with a light and amusing touch. **Amiri Baraka, Poet, Playwright, Activist,**

About the Author

At 71 years old, Horace Mungin has joined the ranks of elders who stand ahead lighting the way for those who follow. He illuminates our time with his wit and insights; his experiences and his understandings. His work has been a beacon to a small band of readers and writers who have made the discovery of his talent. The author encouraged many young poets and writers in his tradition of patients and excellence, and to hold to the belief that it is not through popularity, but a life-long literary journey that the greatest self-satisfaction unfolds.

The poems in this book were written over a forty-seven year period, between 1965 and 2012. They have been arranged into two sections. The first section is called *The Reconstruction,* and it contains poems that were written after 1979; a period when the author's outlook on the question of racial justice was modified by the changes the Civil Rights laws of the sixties was spawning in the country. The second section is called *The Insurrection;* this section contains poems expressed in aggressive petitions for black liberation and racial justice - the passionate radical flames of the author's youth.

The poems in this collection are interesting, well written and provocative, but what makes this a noteworthy collection is that the reader can follow the revolution that took place over a forty year period. The moderation in the later poems can be directly traced to the (sometimes hard to identify) racial moderation still taking place in America. Great poetry masterly interpreted by the drawings of artist Hampton R. Olfus Jr. makes this a must have book.

Made in the USA
Columbia, SC
13 March 2020